Exploring

THE SOUTHWESTERN UNITED STATES

Rose Blue and Corinne J. Naden

Raintree

Chicago, Illinois

Published by Raintree,
a division of Reed Elsevier, Inc.
Chicago, Illinois

For information, address the publisher:

Raintree
100 N. LaSalle
Suite 1200
Chicago IL 60602

07 06 05 04 03
10 9 8 7 6 5 4 3 2 1

Library of Congress Cataloging-in-Publication Data:

Blue, Rose.
  Exploring the southwestern United States / Rose
Blue and Corinne J.Naden.
    v. cm. -- (Exploring the Americas)
Includes bibliographical references (p.   ) and index.
Contents: Marcos de Niza: the golden cities that were
not there (1539) -- Francisco Vasquez de Coronado: in
search of the greatest prize (1540-42) -- Juan
Rodriquez Cabrillo: traveling the coast of California
(1542) -- Sebastian Vizcaino: California's first press
agent (1596) -- Juan de Onate: the New Mexico
Colony (1598) -- Junipero Serra: a new kind of
settlement (1769-82) -- Francisco Silvestre Velez de
Escalante and Francisco Dominguez: on the road to
Monterey (1776-77).
  ISBN 0-7398-4954-9 (Library Binding-hardcover) --
  ISBN 1-4109-0336-2 (Paperback)
  1. Southwest, New--Discovery and exploration--
Juvenile literature. 2. Explorers--Southwest, New--
History--Juvenile literature. 3. Explorers--Spain--
History--Juvenile literature. [1. Southwest,
New--Discovery and exploration. 2. Explorers.] I.
Naden, Corinne J. II. Title. III. Series: Blue, Rose.
Exploring the Americas.
  F799.B66 2003
  979'.01--dc21
                2003004057

Acknowledgments
The author and publishers are grateful to the
following for permission to reproduce copyright
material:

Cover photographs by (main) Bettmann/Corbis;
(map) Corbis

pp. 4, 9, 42 The Granger Collection, New York; p. 6
Georgina Bowater/Corbis; p. 8 Annie Griffiths
Belt/Corbis; p. 10 Galen Frysinger; p. 11 David
Muench/Corbis; pp. 12, 14, 34 Bettmann/Corbis;
pp. 16, 32 Hulton Archive/Getty Images; p. 17
Library of Congress; p. 19 Ron Watts/Corbis; pp. 20,
55 Tom Bean/Corbis; pp. 22, 48, 49, 54 North Wind
Picture Archives; pp. 24, 29 San Diego Historical
Society Photograph Collection; pp. 26, 28, 47, 50
Robert Holmes/Corbis; p. 27 George H. H. Huey/
Corbis; p. 31 Galen Rowell/Corbis; p. 36 Joseph
Sohm/ChromoSohm Inc./Corbis; p. 38 Michael
Freeman/Corbis; p. 39 Craig Aurness/Corbis; p. 41
Buddy Mays/Corbis; p. 44 Danny Lehman/Corbis;
p. 45 Jan Butchofsky-Houser/Corbis; p. 46 Philip
James Corwin/Corbis; p. 51 Corbis; p. 57 Scott T.
Smith/Corbis; compass icon Corbis

Photo research by Julie Laffin

Some words are shown in bold,
like **this.** You can find out what they
mean by looking in the Glossary.

Contents

Prologue:
Who Found It?

What were they looking for? What drove the eight people in this book to explore what is now the southwestern United States?

Most of these adventurers were in the service of Spain. Junipero Serra was a **missionary** in the service of the Catholic church. In the early years of European exploration in the Americas, Spain had two main goals. One was to make Christians of any people the explorers found in what they considered to be the New World. This goal was not necessarily a desire of the Spanish royal house. It was dictated by the pope. After Columbus's first voyage in 1492, Spain petitioned Pope Alexander VI. It wanted all rights to any discoveries by Columbus in the New World. The pope, also a Spaniard, agreed.

There was, however, one catch. The people in any "non-Christian western lands" that Spain conquered had to be converted to Christianity. That is why the

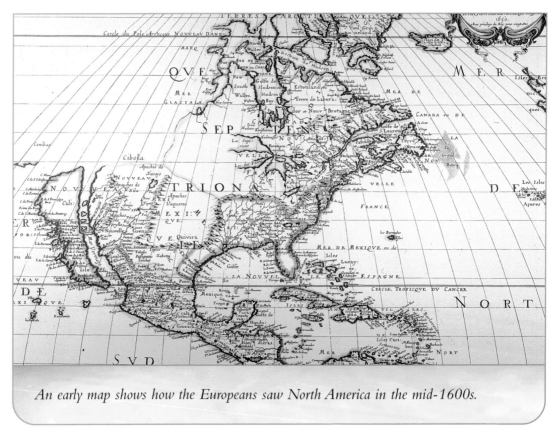

An early map shows how the Europeans saw North America in the mid-1600s.

Spaniards brought along monks and missionaries to convert the people they found there. Spain felt it was bringing religion to people it considered to be heathens, or nonbelievers. On the other hand, Spanish explorers, who were known as conquistadors, meaning "conquerors," were generally a very brutal group. They might have converted the people in such places as Puerto Rico and Cuba, but they also slaughtered entire populations. Sometimes this was done on purpose. Sometimes it happened through ignorance. The Spanish, like other Europeans, crossed the Atlantic and brought with them diseases not found in the Americas. The native populations soon came down with smallpox, measles, and—worst of all—the flu. They had no resistance against these illnesses, so they died by the thousands.

A much more exciting goal for most of the explorers was Spain's other main reason for crossing the Atlantic: Gold! They also came for silver and countless other fabled riches they thought they would find in the Americas. Of course, none of the conquistadors had actually seen these great deposits of wealth. But surely they were there. The native peoples spoke of dazzling empires in Mexico and other areas.

Such tales sent Francisco Vasquez de Coronado off to explore the southwestern United States. Supposedly there were seven Zuni Indian villages with buildings made of gold and turquoise. He found cities, but no gold. However, these expeditions did pave the way for others who traveled to the southwest.

Although adventurers such as these are said to have "discovered" the Grand Canyon, the Rio Grande, or the California coast, of course they did not. These explorers did not really discover anything. All those things were there before the Spanish ventured into the south west. People were living in these territories before Spain, or any of the other European countries, arrived.

What the early explorers did do was record what they saw. Their stories and **journals** expanded the European idea of the world. Their mark is still felt today. Sebastian Vizcaino, for example, traveled up and down the coast of California naming practically everything he saw. Since he had a mapmaker traveling with him, the names stuck. And so we have such places as San Diego, Santa Barbara, and Monterey in California today.

The explorers were brave, reckless, determined, and often greedy, cruel, and ruthless. Those included in this book, with the exception of Junipero Serra, wanted glory for Spain and wealth for themselves. Their journeys changed our world. The records of their travels still read like adventure stories today.

Chapter One

Marcos de Niza
The Golden Cities That Were Not There (1539)

Marcos de Niza (1539–1558) was born in Nice, France. The seaport city is a popular vacation spot today.

In 1539 Franciscan **missionary** and explorer Marcos de Niza wrote, "It is greater than the city of Mexico." He was sitting in the desert in what is now western New Mexico. From a safe distance, he stared at what he claimed to be the Seven Golden Cities of Cibola. They were cities of fabulous wealth and splendor that, according to legend, had been founded by seven Portuguese bishops in the eighth century. The conquistadors, for whom gold always held the greatest attraction, had been looking for these riches ever since. Now, claimed Father Marcos, there they were.

Unfortunately for Marcos, there they were not. Francisco Coronado found that out a year later. But the missionary's false report sent him into disgrace because it led to a major, and expensive, expedition to conquer the golden cities.

Marcos de Niza did not find Cibola because there was no Cibola to find. But he did explore parts of what are now western New Mexico and eastern Arizona. His claims, although false, led to the extraordinary journey of Coronado, which opened southwestern North America to the Europeans.

Getting there

Almost nothing is known about Father Marcos de Niza until he reached the Americas—not his birthdate nor any details of his early life. His birthplace was Nice (Niza in Spanish), France, and that is known only because it is part of his name. He was a missionary in 1531 when he reached the Americas and went to Santo Domingo, Guatemala, and Peru. Reportedly he was present at the capture of the great Inca chief, Atahualpa. He wrote several books that dealt with the conquest of native peoples in South America and became something of an authority on the treatment of these people by the Spanish. From South America, Marcos was sent north into Mexico where he helped to free Indian slaves. In the province of Nueva Galicia, where Francisco Coronado was the governor, the missionary was soon well respected for his work. His travels around the area and into Arizona gave him valuable experience, not only with the Native Americans there, but with the land itself. In 1539 he was named vice commissary-general of the Franciscan Order in New Spain.

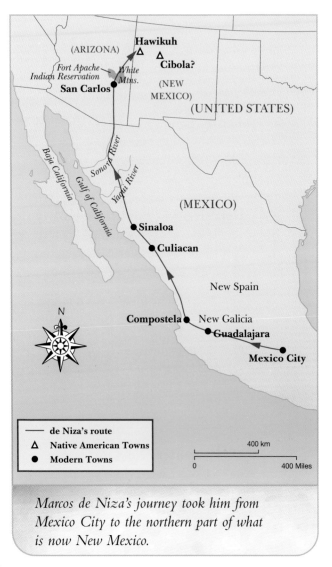

Marcos de Niza's journey took him from Mexico City to the northern part of what is now New Mexico.

Beyond the frontier

His reputation and good works led Father Marcos to a new assignment. The **viceroy** of New Spain, Antonio de Mendoza, chose him to lead an expedition beyond the northern borders of Spain's possessions in North America. He was to verify reports by Alvar Nunez Cabeza de Vaca who was shipwrecked in the region in 1536. Marcos was to search for a civilization in present-day Arizona and New Mexico; specifically the cities of Cibola. Secondly, he was to assure the local native peoples that Spain had nothing but good intentions toward them. This claim would prove to be false.

Marcos left Mexico on March 7, 1539. His **journal** records show that the party traveled the coast of western Mexico to the Yaqui River, then inland and up the Sonora River Valley. After crossing a

The San Pedro River stretches from Cananea, Mexico, to the Gila River near Winkelman, Arizona.

pass to the San Pedro River, he went downstream into present-day Arizona. He led an expedition that included **Friar** Onorato, several Native American interpreters, and the former slave Esteban, who acted as guide. Esteban had been with Cabeza de Vaca on his journey three years earlier. Not long into the expedition, Onorato fell ill and had to be left behind. Marcos was now the only European on the search.

Esteban went on ahead to look for the riches rumored to be in the area. After about four days, he sent back a messenger with some startling news. Esteban had seen seven cities that were "large and wondrous affairs." According to reports, Esteban had been instructed to send a white cross with the messenger. If the cross was as large as the man's hand, that meant news about the fabled cities was good. If the cross was twice that size, the news was even better, and so on. Marcos was delighted when the messenger returned carrying a white cross that was as tall as himself! This was very good news indeed.

Marcos was even more de-lighted when he heard stories from some of the local people about seven rich cities to the north. He prepared for the journey to what he now thought could be the elusive fabled cities. But he was cautious. He did not

Esteban guides de Niza's party in their exploration of the American southwest.

follow Esteban immediately when he heard the news of Cibola. Instead he waited to talk to some Native Americans who had been called from the seacoast. They told him about a wealth of pearls that were found near their homes. Also, their accounts of the cities sounded very much like the message from Esteban.

Finally Marcos set off and followed the markers laid out by Esteban. Along the way he received gifts of fine turquoise and leather from Native Americans in the area. They also spoke of fabulous cities with buildings four and five stories high. Supposedly he even met a Native American who claimed he lived in Cibola. He said the buildings were ten stories high and that the seat of government of the seven cities was Ahacus. This was probably the ruins of Hawikuh, a village of Zuni Native Americans. It is unclear how Marcos could have gotten all these details accurately considering the difficulties of language translation, but more and more, he became convinced that he was pursuing the real thing.

The White Mountain Apache reservation is located in east-central Arizona.

The golden cities

Early in May 1539, Marcos entered the wilderness in and around the present-day White Mountain Apache reservation in Arizona. Many days later he was met by another messenger who informed him that Esteban had been murdered by the Zuni. According to the story, Esteban and some of his guides had been captured by the Zuni and held for three days. When he tried to escape, they were all killed.

By the end of May, Marcos was standing on a hill looking down in the distance at what he thought was Cibola.

He didn't dare to go down and see for himself. He was alone and unarmed. In addition, his Native American guides were getting restless with the talk of Esteban's murder and were threatening to run off. They threatened to kill Marcos as revenge for the death of their friends. The **friar** managed to talk them out of killing him and even persuaded two of them to go with him a little closer to a small hill where he could get a better view of the seven cities. He wrote in his journal that the settlement was larger than the city of Mexico and had a "very fine appearance."

A sotol plant grows near the mountains of Arizona.

not really there. Others have said perhaps the desert atmosphere made the village seem larger than it really was. Whatever the reason, Marcos brought back a glowing account—including the fact that the doorways to the homes in this village were studded with turquoise stones—when he retraced his way to New Spain.

The disgrace

Word quickly spread throughout New Spain that Cibola had been found. Marcos' reputation was greatly enhanced. But it fell just as quickly when Coronado was sent to explore the region in 1540 with Marcos as his guide. Upon close inspection, they found a "mere collection of huts."

Marcos came back to Mexico City in disgrace. His peers even named him the "lying monk." His expeditions through the southwest had also ruined his health. He spent the last fifteen years of his life as an invalid and died in Mexico on March 25, 1558.

Marcos de Niza may not have succeeded in his dream of finding the fabled cities, and his exagerrated reports did cost his government a lot of time and money. Yet he did explore areas in western New Mexico and eastern Arizona that were unknown by the Spanish until that time. And he did pave the way for the remarkable journey of Francisco Coronado.

No one truly knows whether Marcos simply imagined such a magnificent view before him or if he purposely exaggerated his findings for his own glory, or even if the tall tales of the native peoples encouraged him to see what was

Chapter Two
Francisco Vasquez de Coronado
In Search of the Greatest Prize (1540–1542)

Francisco Coronado (c.1510–1554) looked like the picture of a proud conquistador. He sat stiffly on his horse, dressed in gleaming **armor,** his head held erect under a golden helmet. But strictly speaking, Coronado was not a conquistador. That was the name given to early 16th-century adventurers who conquered so much of the so-called New World for Spain. More often than not, they did so in a brutal, violent fashion, as Cortes or Pizarro had a few years earlier. Their main goal had always been gold or other riches. They often put their own glory ahead of Spain's.

Now the king of Spain wanted a new kind of explorer: a man who could lead in battle if necessary but would be loyal to the **crown.** He wanted someone who would not steal the wealth for himself. The king looked for an educated man who would know how to govern the territories that he conquered. Coronado was believed to be such a man.

Francisco Coronado went on a remarkable two-year journey in pursuit of gold. He never found it, but he opened the American southwest for settlers who would follow him into Arizona, New Mexico, Texas, and Oklahoma. He formed relationships with the Pueblo and Apache peoples. His journey opened up almost a quarter of the present-day United States.

A painting by artist Newell Convers Wyeth shows Coronado and his men during "Coronado's March" (1540–1542).

The young nobleman

In about the year 1510, Francisco Vasquez de Coronado was born in the university town of Salamanca, Spain. Unfortunately for him, he was not the firstborn son. Although his family was old and aristocratic, his father was not particularly wealthy. When he died the family estate and properties went to the oldest son. Coronado and his other brothers might enjoy the family name and a good education, but after their father's death, they were on their own.

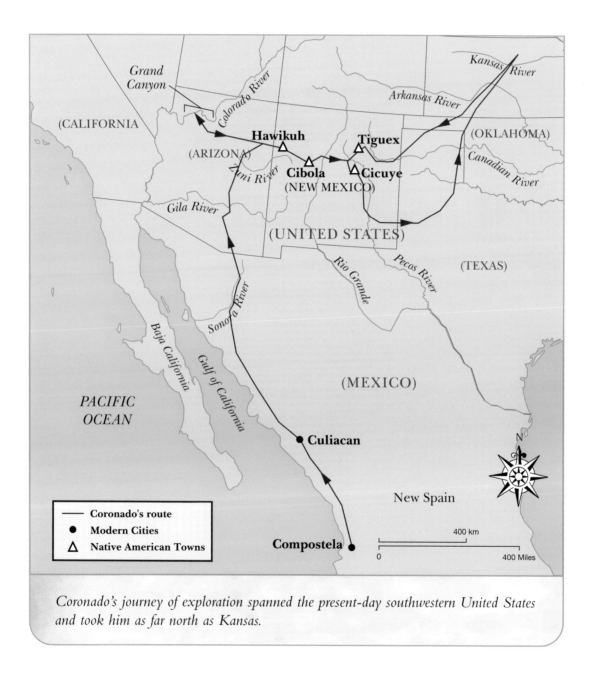

Coronado's journey of exploration spanned the present-day southwestern United States and took him as far north as Kansas.

Coronado and his party follow a Native American guide.

So in 1535 young Coronado sailed to New Spain (Mexico) as one of many aides to Antonio de Mendoza, the **viceroy** of Mexico. Mendoza was supposed to clean up some of the mess created by the conquistadors, especially Cortes. Laws of the Spanish government had to be obeyed. Cruelty to the native peoples was ordered to stop. In fact, the native peoples were supposed to become Spanish citizens, although presumably on the lowest social level.

Coronado advanced his own social level in 1537 by marrying Beatriz, the wealthy daughter of Alonso de Estrada, the former treasurer of New Spain. Estrada's widow gave the young couple a large ranch outside of Mexico City as a wedding gift. Later Coronado and Beatriz founded a home for orphaned girls on ranch land, the first such charitable organization in the New World.

Mendoza obviously liked Coronado and trusted him. He sent the young man to stop an **uprising** by Native Americans working in a silver mine, an assignment that Coronado accomplished with a minimum of deaths. He soon earned a reputation for dealing well with the native peoples. As a reward, he was given a seat on the city council of Mexico, which he would hold until his death. In 1538 Coronado was made governor of Nueva Galicia (present-day Guadalajara). He replaced Nuno de Guzman, who was charged with cruel and corrupt rule and sent back to Spain. Now 28 years old, Coronado took his wife and young daughter and left Mexico City for Compostela, the capital city of Nueva Galicia. This was a heavy responsibility for a young family man.

The lure of gold

For some time Spaniards had heard stories of the fabled seven golden cities of Cibola. This was regarded as the greatest wealth, the richest prize to be found in the New World. It was just a legend. There was no proof that such a prize existed. But this was America in the 1500s and 1600s. It was easy to believe that cities made of gold or fountains with magical powers could be discovered in this huge, unfamiliar, and largely unexplored land. In 1536 four survivors of a Spanish expedition in Florida had found their way to Mexico after a long and dangerous **trek.** They told Mendoza that natives spoke of fabulously rich cities to be found in what is now New Mexico.

Their story intrigued Mendoza, an intelligent but cautious man. And when Marcos de Niza returned with his report of having sighted the seven cities in 1539, Mendoza relaxed his normal caution and planned an expedition. Instead of famed conquistador Hernan Cortes, who might have been a logical choice, he chose young Coronado for the job. Cortes was so upset by this decision that he sailed to Spain to complain to the king. As it turned out, Cortes later probably thought it fortunate that he had been turned down. As for Coronado, this was his chance to find the richest of all prizes for his country. With this expedition he could become Spain's greatest hero.

Toward a legend

Mendoza decided on a practical approach to find the golden cities. He would send two forces, the major one by land and a smaller force by sea. Coronado would lead the land force. The sea expedition under command of Hernando de Alarcon, with one ship and one **sloop,** would sail north and keep in touch with the land march if possible. Alarcon did sail up the Gulf of California and proved that Lower California was a peninsula, not an island. He also found the mouth of the Colorado River, but he did not meet the land force as hoped.

Expeditions such as these cost a lot of money, even by 16th-century standards. To help pay for them, some of the soldiers donated their own money, as did many Spanish citizens in Mexico. They hoped for a share of the great riches that would be found. Coronado donated a large sum of his wife's money as well. The expedition to find the seven cities probably cost many millions of dollars by today's economics.

Coronado said goodbye to his wife and left Compostela late in February 1540. Marcos de Niza was his guide. Riding his

Coronado's expedition crosses the plains of Kansas on his search for the legendary Seven Cities of Cibola.

horse and clad in gleaming **armor** and a golden helmet, Coronado led some 300 Spanish soldiers from the city. The expedition also included hundreds of Indian guides, some of them slaves, four priests, one surgeon, and herds of pigs, sheep, and cattle.

With all those people, animals, and supplies, travel was slow. There were also several minor skirmishes with native peoples. Then Coronado received some startling news from a scout returning from the north region. He said that the stories of the golden cities were false. The scout also claimed that the region was home to hostile native peoples who would fight any intruders. Marcos de Niza contradicted the report, declaring that the scout was wrong. The expedition

proceeded, but now Coronado began to have some doubts about the priest's story.

A major disaster occurred on the trail soon after. In a Native American ambush, Coronado's trusted and valuable second in command was killed. It then took an entire month to reach Culiacan, the northernmost Spanish post in Mexico. From there the expedition had to travel another 800 miles (1,287 kilometers) to reach Cibola. Already dismayed at the slow pace of the march, Coronado decided to split the expedition into two groups. He would go ahead with a force of about 80 soldiers and 200 Native Americans. Marcos would go with him, and the rest of the expedition would proceed at a slower pace.

Marcus assured Coronado that now the traveling would be easy. It definitely was not. Many of the horses lost their footing on the steep mountain cliffs. Food was scarce because it was spring, and the Native Americans were just planting crops, not harvesting them. As Coronado moved north into Arizona, water was hard to find and many of the animals died. There were attacks by hostile native peoples. They encountered rattlesnakes and huge lizards known as gila monsters, which are native to the southwestern United States. Finally, after a long and torturous **trek** through

Ruins are all that remain of the pueblos that the Zuni people once lived in.

the desert region, Coronado reached the Zuni River where it flows from New Mexico into Arizona. According to the reports of Marcos, he was near Cibola.

On the morning of July 7, 1540, a tired and thirsty group of Spanish soldiers looked down on their destination. Where were the riches described by Marcos? Coronado could only shake his head in dismay. Instead of the golden cities of Cibola, he saw only **adobe** houses clustered close together, just like in poor cities anywhere.

The dream of a fortune in gold was fast fading. So was Coronado's own fortune, since he had sunk so much of his wife's money into the expedition. Fading, too, was his dream of recognition as a great and victorious leader.

Coronado was soon jolted out of his depression by a more pressing problem than the loss of gold. Dressed in his full **armor** and representing the **crown** of Spain, he stepped forward to greet the Zuni people of the village. They answered him with a shower of arrows. Coronado had no choice but to attack. In the ensuing fight, the Zuni at first seemed to be winning since they could hide behind the adobe walls for protection. The Spanish had to fight out in the open. Coronado himself was a fine target as he dashed around with his golden armor glittering and his sword cutting flashes in the desert sun. It was easy for the Zuni to drop rocks on his head from the top of the adobe houses. Coronado was knocked unconscious and, although he was wounded, his sturdy helmet saved his life.

He woke to find that the Spanish had rallied and the Zuni had surrendered. Coronado allowed them to leave Cibola. He claimed the region for the king of Spain and sent his men searching through the **pueblo** for signs of gold treasure. They found none. But they did find something almost as important at the moment—food.

Still the truth had to be faced. Cibola was a myth. Coronado sent Marcos back to Mexico with the report.

Cibola was actually a Zuni pueblo, or village, called Hawikah. There were supposedly seven such villages in a small radius, although present-day archaeologists have uncovered only six. They were known by the collective name of Cibola.

While Coronado recovered from his wound, he and his men settled down in the pueblo where they lived for several months. During that period, some of the Zuni moved back into the village and got along quite well with the Spanish. Coronado sent a letter to Mendoza by messenger. He praised his men but admitted the expedition was a failure. There was no gold. The legend of the golden cities was a lie after all.

The next golden tale

In the letter to Mendoza, Coronado said that he was going to continue the expedition by sending scouting parties around the region. Perhaps he still held a glimmer of hope that the golden cities did in fact exist. He sent Captain Melchor Diaz to meet Alarcon who had taken the sea route. By now Alarcon had returned to Mexico because he could not find Coronado's party. Like Alarcon, Diaz reached the Colorado River but he died from a fall off his horse.

In an effort to find out more about possible riches, Coronado visited the other Zuni pueblos in the area, but found no wealth. However, the Native Americans suggested that a village called Quivira to the northeast (present-day central Kansas) might be what he sought.

Before going in that direction, Coronado sent a small scouting party, led by Captain Pedro de Tovar, to the northwest. After a journey of about 150 miles (241 kilometers), Tovar met the Hopi Indians of northeastern Arizona. Like the Zuni they lived in pueblos clustered into a number of independent towns. After a brief hostile encounter, calm was restored between the two groups, and the Hopi told Tovar about a great river to the west. Tovar returned to Coronado with the news.

Coronado sent another party to investigate beyond the land of the Hopi. This time Garcia Lopez de Cardenas led his men into northwestern Arizona where they came upon an unbelievable sight. Cardenas and his men were reportedly the first Europeans to see the Grand Canyon. This immense gorge cut by the Colorado River is one mile (1.5 kilometers) deep, as much as 18 miles (29 kilometers) wide, and extends a distance of about 277 miles (446 kilometers). No other place on earth compares with the Grand Canyon for the geological time clock that is exposed on its bare walls. The crystallized rocks of the inner gorge at the bottom of the canyon may be two billion years old. Some overlaying sheets of black lava may be merely 1,000 years old.

When Cardenas returned with his spectacular sighting, Coronado was very impressed but not enough to make the trip himself. He never saw the Grand Canyon. Gold was still the bigger draw.

The world's largest canyon, the Grand Canyon ranges from 0.1 to 18 miles (0.2 to 29 kilometers) across.

Strangely enough, had he made the trip to the Grand Canyon and westward, he might have found what he was seeking. He may not have seen a golden city, but California, as it was later discovered, really did turn out to be a gold mine.

Coronado's search for gold now turned to the east. He met a leader from the village of Cicuye, near modern-day Santa Fe, New Mexico. Because of the hair on his lip, the Spaniards called him "Bigotes," which means mustache or whiskers. Bigotes told Coronado about Tigeux, which he described as a wonderland. He also spoke of strange humpback creatures (**buffalo**). Coronado sent

Hernando de Alvarado with Bigotes to explore the area, which was about 170 miles (274 kilometers) east. Once again there was no gold, but Alvarado did find the wide river called the Rio Grande. Noting the rich fertile farmland, Alvarado sent back a message that this would be an ideal spot for the Spaniards to spend the winter.

While waiting for Coronado's answer, Alvarado asked Bigotes to travel farther east with him to see the humpback animals. Instead, Bigotes sent along a young Native American slave who knew the area well. Because the slave wore a turban on his head, which the

Buffalo, once common on the plains of the present-day United States, were a very strange sight for early European explorers.

Spaniards thought resembled men in Turkey, they called him El Turco (The Turk). As it turned out, The Turk was almost as good at making up stories as Marcos de Niza had been. And both men completely fooled Coronado.

On to Quivira

The Turk did indeed take Alvarado to the great herds of buffalo on the plains. He also told him of a wondrous place on a mighty river to the northeast. This was Quivira in modern-day central Kansas. The fish in the river were as large as horses, said the Turk. He claimed that gold was everywhere,

decorating the large boats rowed by many oarsmen on the waters. The people lived in impressive houses and gold trinkets hung from the trees. Everyone ate from golden dishes and drank from silver goblets. Alvarado was quite impressed by these stories.

Why did these otherwise bold and hardy soldiers seem so willing to believe these seemingly ridiculous stories? For one thing, very little was known about this strange new world. Just seeing a buffalo was an unbelievable experience! If such an odd animal existed, why not a place where gold trinkets hang from trees? It also may be that the Spaniards truly wanted so much to believe in a fabulous golden city that they accepted such stories without thinking too much about their credibility.

When Alvarado returned to Bigotes, he asked him about the land of Quivira. Bigotes said the Turk was crazy or a liar. The people of Quivira lived in rough huts just like everyone else, Bigotes said, and there was no gold.

But once the lure of fabulous riches takes hold, otherwise sane men can act in strange and terrible ways. Alvarado chained Bigotes and took him back to Coronado, who had moved his army to winter headquarters in Tigeux. When Bigotes refused to say that gold existed at Quivira and repeatedly said such stories were false, Coronado allowed him to be tortured. This was unlike Coronado, who was noted as a fair and just man. Perhaps he just had to believe that the gold existed. But it cost him dearly. When the Native Americans saw the chieftain being tortured, they revolted and a terrible fight broke out.

There were two major battles during that winter of 1540–1541. At the end of one of them, the Spaniards tied about 30 Native Americans to posts and burned them to death as warning to the others. The order for the burning was given by Cardenas, the soldier who had been to the Grand Canyon. He was later tried and sent to prison back in Spain.

Although Coronado did not personally give the order to deal with the Native Americans in such a barbaric way, he did not punish Cardenas for doing so.

Coronado was known as an honorable man, but he committed a very dishonable act for his handling of the native peoples. He lost their respect and he would later lose the respect of his country as well.

The search for gold had become an obsession with the young Spaniard. With the Turk's urging, he was totally convinced that Quivira was the prize. In the spring of 1541, Coronado moved his force into Palo Duro Canyon in Texas. There they saw the great buffalo herds. Then, with most of the force returning to Tiguex, Coronado and 30 of his best horsemen set out for the northeast.

It took more than a month for Coronado to reach his latest dream of gold. At last it stood before him—Quivira. The Turk had said it was a place of impressive homes, rich people, and golden trinkets hanging from the trees. What Coronado saw were grass huts, poor Native Americans, and no trinkets of any kind. Bigotes had been telling the truth. Quivira was just another poor Native American **pueblo.**

A disillusioned Coronado returned to Tiguex, but not before he formally claimed the region for the king of Spain. He questioned the Turk and discovered that he had always planned to deceive the Spaniards. The Turk was strangled for his deception.

Since winter was now setting in, Coronado decided to remain in Tiguex. Two days after Christmas, he fell while exercising his horse and was kicked in the head. The accident was caused by a rotting leather band that held his saddle. The injury was so severe that he spent days in a coma. Coronado did survive, but the young leader was never quite the same, physically or mentally. Possibly he had suffered brain damage as a result of the head injury. Sometimes he was quiet, withdrawn, and almost fearful. Sometimes he seemed nearly his old, confident self.

The journey home

Now in ill health, Coronado could fool himself no longer. There were no golden cities in this strange new land. Fearing that he would soon die of his injury, Coronado finally admitted defeat and decided to return to Mexico. One of the priests, Juan de Padilla, and two other **missionaries** asked to be allowed to return to Quivira to administer to the Native Americans. Coronado agreed. Padilla later became the first Christian missionary to be martyred in the land that became the United States.

Father Juan de Padilla accompanied Coronado on his search for Quivira.

Coronado let the priests go but denied the request of several of his soldiers to remain. These young men had found the fertile farmlands of Kansas a good place to live, even without the golden trinkets. But Coronado ordered all his soldiers to return with him. So it was that in the spring of 1542, Francisco Coronado, ill and disillusioned, led his ragtag group of soldiers back to Mexico. It was an exhausting journey of 900 miles (1,448 kilometers). On some days, Coronado could ride his horse, on others he had to be carried in a litter. The once proud army that had left Mexico to pursue a dream of gold was filthy, tired, and discouraged.

They reached Culiacin in June. Then Coronado went on to Mexico City, but much of his army did not accompany him. Fearing that they would be punished for their failure, many of them simply disappeared, choosing to live their lives in obscurity in northern Mexico.

The defeated warrior presented himself to Mendoza in Mexico City. He had to admit that the expedition was a failure and that all the money given by Mendoza and other Spaniards was lost. Whatever Mendoza's reaction, Coronado was allowed to resume his governorship of Nueva Galicia and was also allowed to retain his seat as a royal official.

Two years later an official inquiry was brought against Coronado by the Mexican *audiencia,* the governing body in the Spanish colonies. This was a routine action for any expedition leader. Coronado was accused of brutality against the Native Americans. He was fined and lost a number of valuable possessions from his estate. But in 1546 a panel led by Mendoza found him innocent of all charges.

For eight years, Coronado and his wife lived in Mexico City. He became more ill and died on September 22, 1554, at the age of 44. Coronado was buried beneath the altar of the Church of Santo Domingo in Mexico City.

In one way, Coronado can be considered a failure. He never achieved his goal. On the other hand, he could not have achieved it because what he sought did not exist. There never were cities made of gold in the New World. Like many others, Coronado was following a foolish dream. He probably thought of himself as a failure as well. Yet his expeditions actually accomplished a great deal. He and his men had traveled the Colorado, Kansas, and Arkansas Rivers. They had explored much of the western lands north of Mexico and were the first Europeans to see the Grand Canyon. Coronado's journeys answered many questions about the unknown southwestern region of North America. Because of his travels in a fruitless quest, he opened the way for thousands of settlers into what became the great southwest of the United States.

Chapter Three

Juan Rodriguez Cabrillo
Traveling the Coast of California (1542)

The first European to see the south-western coast of North America was a Portuguese explorer in the service of Spain. His account of the expedition marked the beginning of recorded history in what would become the 31st state of the United States of America. The explorer was Juan Rodriguez Cabrillo (c.1500–1543) and the state was California. His journeys to Central America and the Pacific coast were motivated, like most of the explorers of his era, by the promise of great wealth. In this case, he achieved it by finding gold in Coban, Guatemala, in the 1520s, which made him a rich man.

A man of mystery

Little is known about Cabrillo's early years, including when and where he was born. His birthdate was probably about 1500 or a year or two earlier, since he was in his early twenties when he left for the Americas in 1520. Most scholars believe he was born in Portugal, although some say he was Spanish. In either case, he sailed for Spain.

The first recorded word of Cabrillo appears in 1520 when the young soldier accompanied Panfilo de Narvaez to Mexico. Narvaez was sent to the New World to control the ambitious Hernan Cortes, brutal conqueror of the Aztecs

Juan Rodriguez Cabrillo (c.1500–1543)

in Mexico. Narvaez was unsuccessful in his mission, and Cabrillo seems to have switched allegiance to Cortes. Cabrillo was apparently part of the final assault on the Aztec capital of Tenochtitlan on August 13, 1520. He was wounded during the battle, in which he fought as a captain of soldiers armed with crossbows.

In 1523 Cabrillo was evidently one of the conquerors in the Spanish conquest of what are now Guatemala, El Salvador, and Nicaragua in Central America. He was probably part of the expeditions of Pedro de Alvarado. Cabrillo stayed in Guatemala where he was listed as a registered citizen by 1532. For a while he may have been the region's governor and was certainly the leading citizen of Santiago, Guatemala's principal town at the time.

As a reward for services to the **crown,** the king of Spain granted encomiendas, or long-term leases on land use with the right to employ forced Native American labor for such projects. Cabrillo received a number of encomiendas, and as a result of mining for gold in Guatemala, he became quite rich.

Cabrillo returned to Spain in 1532, where he married Beatriz Sanchez de Ortega. They would later have two sons. When Cabrillo and his wife returned to Guatemala the following year, he was made an official of the port city of Iztapa, south of Santiago. He was also asked to build a fleet of ships for Alvarado's proposed expedition to the Spice Islands. Cabrillo would later sail one of those ships, the *San Salvador,* on his own expedition to California.

For some time the Spanish **viceroy** of Mexico, Antonio de Mendoza, had been sending out expeditions to search for gold and claim new lands for the crown. He had sent Marcos de Niza and

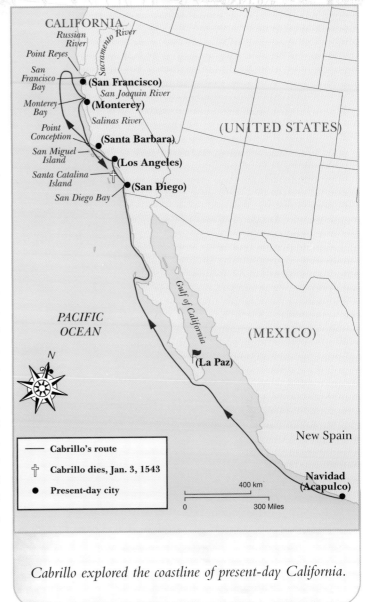

Cabrillo explored the coastline of present-day California.

Francisco Coronado on what turned out to be fruitless searches for the golden cities. He also sent a fleet across the Pacific to the Philippine Islands. In 1542 he chose Cabrillo to lead an expedition along the Pacific coast north of Mexico to look for new land.

Cabrillo was the first European to visit Point Concepcion.

On June 17, 1542, Cabrillo left a Mexican port near present-day Acapulco with three ships carrying supplies for a two-year voyage. He sailed north along the western coast of Mexico and crossed the Gulf of California until, on or about July 2, he reached Baja California. This is the long narrow peninsula that juts southward from the state of California. The Spanish already knew about Baja California from earlier expeditions sent out by Cortes. The name "California" came from the name of an island in a story written by Garcia Rodriguez de Montalvo and published in about 1510. The mythical island was ruled by Queen Califia, ruler of the Amazons, a race of women warriors.

Despite earlier Spanish expeditions, Cabrillo was the first European to make actual contact with the native peoples of Baja California. From there he sailed north again along the western coast of Baja, arriving at a small sheltered **bay** in September. Supposedly he named it San Diego Bay for the smallest of his three ships. Some historians, however, say he called the bay San Miguel and the name was changed by a later explorer, Sebastian Vizcaino. Cabrillo named just about every **bay** and inlet that he saw, and some of the names remain. Sailing north once more, he met and talked with many of the native peoples along the coast. He found them all to be friendly and willing to trade. The first group he met were fishermen, and they told him about other Native Americans who lived inland and grew maize (corn).

When Cabrillo sailed just north of present-day Los Angeles, he came upon a large Native American village. He landed and took possession of the region in the name of the Spanish king. In October he sailed into what is now Santa Barbara where he traded with the friendly Chumash people. Passing through the Santa Barbara **Channel,** he stopped at a number of islands, including Santa Catalina, which he supposedly called San Salvador after his **flagship.** He also gave the name of Victoria, after another of his ships, to present-day San Clemente.

After exploring the islands, Cabrillo got back to the mainland at Point Conception, but there he ran into heavy storms. The weather was so bad that he missed both Monterey and San Francisco **bays** entirely. These were places where he certainly could have found shelter. Instead he kept on sailing

San Miguel Island is 55 miles (89 kilometers) off the coast of Ventura, California. It is the farthest west of the Channel Islands.

to a point about 50 miles (80 kilometers) north of San Francisco at the Russian River. He then turned south and anchored at San Miguel, another island in the Santa Barbara **Channel,** to spend the winter.

After all his navigation of strange and sometimes dangerous waters, Cabrillo ran into trouble while waiting out the winter on San Miguel. During a Native American attack, he broke his leg. Complications set in, and Juan Cabrillo died on January 3, 1543. His second in command, Bartolome Ferrelo, took charge of the expedition. On January 19 Ferrelo decided to sail north but bad weather forced him back. Still determined, he headed farther out to sea before turning north again. He sighted land at Point Arena, which is about 100 miles (161 kilometers) north of San Francisco. He rounded Cape Mendocino and reached the Rogue River in southern Oregon on March 1. On the trip back, Ferrelo's two ships were separated by storms but both reached Navidad harbor safely on April 14, 1543.

A failure for a while

Cabrillo's expedition was considered a failure at the time. It brought no immediate benefits to Spain or New Spain. It was not until the next century that explorers would bring the western coast into the Spanish empire. Although it was not published until the 1800s, Cabrillo's account of the voyage is the oldest written record of human activity

A monument to Cabrillo stands in San Diego, California.

on the west coast. His voyage opened the way for the next round of explorers and helped to dispel myths and misconceptions about that part of the so-called New World.

Cabrillo Point at the entrance to San Diego Harbor is named in honor of the explorer. U.S. President Woodrow Wilson acknowledged his contribution by authorizing the Cabrillo National Monument in 1913. A statue of the explorer looks out over the bay that he first entered in September 1542.

Chapter Four
Sebastian Vizcaino
California's First Press Agent (1596)

If a press agent is someone hired to publicize the merits of a person or place, then it is just possible that Sebastian Vizcaino (c.1550–c.1628) was California's first press agent. He might also have been the first press agent to exaggerate what he saw. He returned to Mexico with such glowing descriptions of Monterey Bay that later explorers did not even recognize it.

The merchant-explorer

Sebastian Vizcaino was born in Spain around 1550, probably in the town of Corcho. His family had no royal titles, but he might have served in Portugal's royal army in 1567. By 1585 he was involved in the sea trade to China, making at least one voyage to Manila between 1586 and 1589. It is known that he was unlucky enough to be a passenger aboard the treasure **galleon** *Santa Ana* on November 14, 1587. That was the ship sighted by the famous English navigator and rogue, Thomas Cavendish. The third man to sail around the world, Cavendish took special delight in attacking Spanish ships and settlements whenever possible. On that day he seized and burned the *Santa Ana* off the coast of California. Although Vizcaino and the other passengers made

A portait depicts Sebastian Vizcaino (c.1550–c.1628).

it back to shore, they did so without much of their fortunes.

Vizcaino returned to Mexico and by 1593 had recovered enough to form a company for explorations. He apparently told the **viceroy** in New Spain that his plans were to explore California to keep it safe from enemies, to bring religion to the poor native peoples, and to find the **Straits** of Anian. (It was said that both the English and the French had sailed through these elusive **straits** on their way to the Pacific. They were never found but are probably today's Bering Strait in Alaska.) However, the real motive behind Vizcaino's new venture could possibly have been the fact that he had heard the region was rich in pearls. Whether the Spanish **crown** realized the true mission or not, it approved Vizcaino's request. There was general unrest among Native Americans at the time, so Spanish ships in the area probably seemed like a good idea. Vizcaino received a commission to search the pearl **fisheries** in Baja California and also to explore the California coast.

He sent out the first expedition from Mexico in 1594 with Perez del Castillo in command. Castillo made such a mess of the voyage that he returned to face criminal charges. But the crown found Vizcaino innocent of any connection with the crimes and gave him another contract. This time he hired himself. He sailed from Acapulco with three ships and 230 men in June 1596. But after a few months of no pearls and exploring nothing of interest, he returned to Acapulco in December.

On to Monterey

With two failed expeditions behind him, Vizcaino probably decided to plan a little more thoroughly for the next trip. It was not until May 5, 1602, that he was ready to sail with a full crew, including experienced navigators, map-

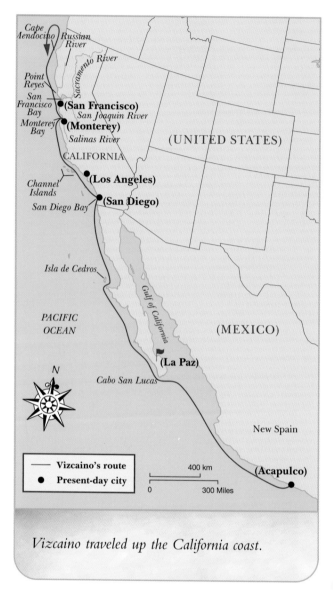

Vizcaino traveled up the California coast.

makers, and **missionaries.** They left Acapulco in three vessels and with specific instructions from the **viceroy** of New Spain. Vizcaino was to explore the California coast to Cape Mendocino especially looking for good harbors and trying to find the Anian straits.

Baja California is a spot known for high winds off the coast almost any time of the year, and Vizcaino quickly ran into them. He did not reach San Diego **Bay** until November. The fact that Vizcaino had very competent mapmakers with him accounts for part of his press-agent fame. He stopped at the same points visited by Cabrillo years earlier and renamed many of them, even though he was told not to do so. But the maps were very accurate for the time and were widely circulated. The names became permanent, such as San Diego, Santa Catalina, Santa Barbara, Monterey, and San Buenaventura.

After some rest and ship repairs, Vizcaino set out to the north. On December 15, he recorded his discovery of Monterey Bay, which Cabrillo had missed. Actually Vizcaino was not the first European to see the bay. It had been first sighted seven years earlier on an expedition by Portuguese adventurer

Monterey Bay was named for the viceroy of Mexico, Conde de Monterey.

Sebastian Cermeno. Nonetheless, Vizcaino named the **bay** for the **viceroy** in New Spain, the Conde de Monterey.

Life would have been easier for the next explorers if they had followed Cermeno's description of Monterey Bay instead of Vizcaino's. Probably feeling that he had better return with a successful expedition because of the two previous failures, Vizcaino described Monterey Bay in terms that had little to do with reality. It was, he said, "the best harbor that could be desired." It was "sheltered from all winds," which was news to all those who later explored it since Monterey Bay has no proper harbor at all. It was also, according to Vizcaino, favored with good amounts of timber, water, and other wood. In fact, his description was so glowing that most of the adventurers who followed Vizcaino's reports didn't recognize Monterey Bay when they got there.

A Spanish galleon, like those used in Vizcaino's time, sets out to sea.

Vizcaino did include in his report that the native peoples spoke of much gold to be found in the interior. That, of course, is the one thing Vizcaino reported that should have been taken as real fact! (Centuries later, in 1848, gold was discovered at Sutter's Mill in the hills of California, and the Gold Rush was on.) After Monterey Vizcaino ran into all the hardships of any early expedition, such as bad weather, bad food, and the often fatal illness called scurvy. At one point he had to send one of the vessels back to New Spain carrying all those who were ill. Two ships reached Cape Mendocino on January 12, 1603. He also missed San Francisco Bay because of bad weather. With the two remaining ships badly battered, Vizcaino decided to return to New Spain, which he did in February. Half of the crew died on that expedition, mainly from scurvy, but the voyage was pronounced a great success. That is probably because the viceroy was very pleased to have such a splendid bay named after him.

A new viceroy

Vizcaino told the viceroy that a port should be built at Monterey to protect New Spain from its enemies and to refit the Spanish **galleons** returning from Manila in the Philippines. He even sailed to Spain to plead his case before the Council of the Indies. A royal decree was granted to build the port of Monterey with Vizcaino in charge.

Unfortunately for Vizcaino, Viceroy Monterey was then appointed to Peru and the Marques de Montesclaros took his place in New Spain. The new viceroy was jealous of his predecessor's success. He declared himself opposed to the idea of using California as a stopping point for the Spanish galleons coming from the Far East. So Montesclaros authorized a search for nonexistent North Pacific islands instead. He insisted that Monterey could be too easily captured by Spain's enemies. He also said that California was useless as a port of call since it was so close to Mexico anyway. He was correct about that, because even 150 years later when Alta (Upper) California was finally settled, ships from Manila rarely stopped there.

As for Vizcaino, Montesclaros distrusted him and refused to give him command of a galleon for Manila as promised by Monterey. In fact, Montesclaros accused Vizcaino's main mapmaker of **forgery** and had him hanged.

The last years

This jealousy, bickering, and distrust resulted in California being abandoned by Spain for about 150 years. It also shows how little the Spaniards thought of what was eventually to be realized as a fabulously rich prize. They believed California was a place with no gold and a dangerous coast. All the danger and trouble just getting to and from Mexico to California did not seem worth it.

As compensation for not getting the galleon he had been promised, Vizcaino was given command of an expedition in 1611. He was sent to find two islands, Rica de Oro and Rica de Plata, which were supposed to lie somewhere near Japan. No such islands were found and Vizcaino returned to Mexico in January 1614. Nothing is known of his life from then until his death, which occurred around 1628.

Vizcaino may have exaggerated what he saw for his personal gain, but he did provide a great service to Spain. His was the first scientific exploration of the western coast and the maps of his voyage were remarkable for the time.

Chapter Five
Juan de Onate
The New Mexico Colony (1598)

Juan de Onate (c.1550–1626) is surely the forgotten explorer. His name is missing from most histories of the southwest. Or at least he gets no more than a footnote. This conquistador established the colony of New Mexico for Spain, but most New Mexicans have never heard of him. Neither have many people in Spain or Mexico itself. There are many stories about Coronado or Cortes, but few of Onate. Yet he played an important, if brief, role in the development of the American southwest.

More businessman than adventurer, but a harsh and often brutal dictator, Juan de Onate formally established the colony of New Mexico in 1598. Like most of the conquistadors, he was mostly after gold.

Onate was born around the year 1550 in North America, probably in the frontier settlement of Zacatecas, Mexico. He was the son of Catalina de Salazar and Cristobal de Onate, a wealthy mine owner. As a young man he led campaigns against the Chichimec Indians. Juan added to the family prestige when he married Isabel de Tolosa Cortes Montezuma. Her father was Leonor Montezuma, a descendant of the Aztec emperor, and she was also a granddaughter of famous conquistador Hernan Cortes, a marriage between the two families having taken place some years earlier.

To New Mexico

By 1595 Onate was a successful and wealthy silver miner. But he hungered for more and for the honor that could come only from the Spanish king. So he

A portrait shows Juan de Onate (c.1550–1626) exploring New Mexico.

asked for and was awarded a contract from King Philip II on September 21, 1595. The Spanish king was getting a little more cautious about handing out contracts to conquistadors, who often exploited the Native Americans and brought back more trouble than wealth. Onate was given permission to establish a colony in what would be called New Mexico. The stated purpose was to con-vert the native peoples to Christianity, which generally meant subduing any violence, and to give Spain a secure foothold in the western part of North America. Onate was kind of a contract developer in this arrangement, using some of his own fortune to finance the expedition. Naturally, he expected to get it all back in the form of gold or silver and in a share of the tax revenue

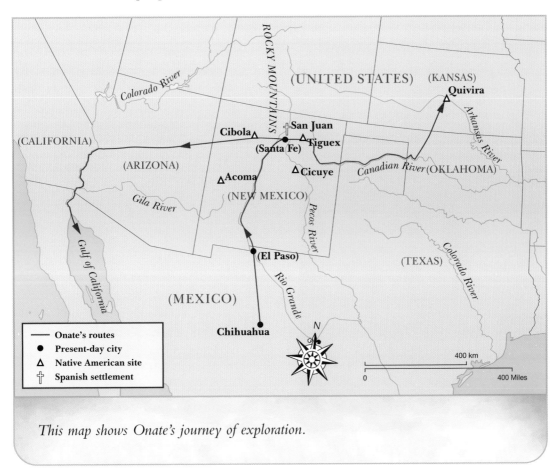

This map shows Onate's journey of exploration.

that the new colony would produce. He thought he would also undoubtedly receive a title or two for his achievement.

It took three years before the expedition was ready. In January 1598 Onate left the settlement of Chihuahua heading north to the Rio Grande. With him was a party of approximately 600 people. This group was made up of soldiers, Native American guides, slaves, 8 priests, 2 lay brothers, and about 400 settlers, including several dozen women and children. The caravan stretched for about 4 miles with 83 wagons and about 7,000 animals.

At 1,900 miles (3,060 kilometers), the Rio Grande is the fifth-longest river in North America.

Three months later the procession arrived at the Rio Grande at what is now El Paso, Texas. Onate named it El Paso del Rio del Norte (ford of the river of the north). The city of El Paso is one of the few places in the United States that remember Onate. In fact, the city celebrates his crossing the Rio Grande at El Paso on the last weekend of April. A bronze statue was dedicated in his honor in downtown El Paso in 1998.

With the help of the friendly Manso people in the area, Onate and his caravan crossed the river into what is now New Mexico. He formally took possession of the land for Spain on April 30, 1598. To give thanks for their safe arrival, the settlers celebrated with a huge feast. By late May Onate came into contact with the many Native American **pueblos** in the northern Rio Grande valley. By July he had established his headquarters for the New Mexico colony at San Juan Pueblo, in present-day Rio Arriba County north of Santa Fe. The colony was named after the prophet St. John the Baptist. There is little left today of the original Spanish settlement. The church, which was quickly erected, is long gone and the settlers' quarters are covered by centuries of river silt. Onate chose the site mainly because any attackers would have to cross the river to get to the colony.

The Native Americans were probably more curious than alarmed at first when the Spaniards appeared on their horses with Onate and the soldiers decked out in velvet and **armor.** The sight of all their guns and **artillery,** however, could not have been reassuring. But Onate had more important things to deal with at first. Even though the settlers were supposed to be building a colony, most of them thought they would become rich on the treasures reported to be in the area. When they found only dust and poor Native Americans, about half of them threatened a mutiny. Onate handled that by immediately executing two of the ringleaders.

The first colony

The other main purpose of Onate's colony was supposedly to bring Christianity—in the form of Catholicism —to the native peoples. Whether true or not, this was nearly always a stated purpose for Spanish expeditions, which is why priests and **missionaries** generally went along. Before the business of **conversion** could be started, however, Onate sent out small parties to scout the area in search of treasure. Onate himself went to Hopi and Zuni pueblos in the far west. Some of the scouts explored to the east and to the Texas border, perhaps near present-day Amarillo. One group went to the San Francisco mountains in Arizona, where they did find some silver ore. In general the parties returned without gold or silver or any other treasure. They simply did not exist in the surrounding area. At this point, troubles began. With no hope of getting rich, many of the would-be settlers wanted to go home.

Onate then became a dictator, brutal in his treatment of unhappy settlers and native peoples. Several of the settlers were executed. A mission was constructed, but it was not long before Onate and his soldiers ran into trouble with the priests. The two sides seemed to hold differing ideas on what was meant when the king ordered them to "purify the native people of New Mexico by converting them to Christianity." The religious group thought that the order meant education. They adopted a kind of fatherly or big-brother attitude toward the Native Americans—whether they wanted it or not. To Onate and the military, it apparently meant stealing and committing acts of violence. Any signs of revolt or rebellion among settlers or Native Americans were often met with death. Mistreatment of the native peoples reached such a point that the missionaries protested by sending several letters back to Mexico asking that the colony be abandoned to protect the Native Americans.

Onate continued to send scouting parties to look for treasure, partly as a way to pacify the settlers. But none of these journeys produced gold or silver. As he traveled Onate came in contact with many native peoples and demanded their allegiance, or submission, to the king. What often followed were fierce battles, since many Native Americans saw no reason to honor a faraway figure whose religion meant nothing to them. Many were killed for their resistance. A favorite punishment seemed to be cutting off a foot.

Three years passed and there was little to brag about in New Mexico. A church was built but it had few followers. The Native Americans were angry and fearful. Most of the settlers wanted to go home. The colony was ailing. Supplies and reinforcements finally came from Mexico in late 1600, but the misery continued. The harsh winter weather took its toll, and food was often scarce.

The desperate search

In June of 1601, Onate left on another treasure hunt, this time to find the legendary wealth that was supposedly in Quivira (central Kansas). Others, most notably Coronado in 1541, had tried

and failed in this same quest. But the lure of the golden city was too much to resist. Onate followed the Canadian River, crossed the Texas panhandle, and turned to the northeast. Eventually he reached central Kansas and the fabled golden place called Quivira. It was nothing but poor Native American villages in the hot Kansas sun. There was not a golden roof in sight.

Discouraged and emptyhanded, Onate returned to a nearly deserted San Juan **Pueblo.** Most of the settlers had decided that his absence was a good time to run for home. In Onate's reports to the

These pueblos were home to Native Americans for over 300 years.

The city of Santa Fe is now the capital of New Mexico.

viceroy and the king, he had painted glowing pictures of the growth of the colony even though that was far from the truth and he had found no treasure at all. Now, in a desperate attempt to recover his prestige, he made one more expedition in search of gold. It took him west to the Colorado River and south to the Gulf of California. But once again Onate and his 30 soldiers found no gold.

By now the viceroy in Mexico, Montesclaros, had collected a number of reports sent by the priests at San Juan Pueblo. They spoke of misery, starvation, and torture. The viceroy weighed these reports against the glowing letters from Onate with no evidence of treasure. The conquest, wrote the viceroy to the Spanish king, "is becoming a fairy tale." In 1606 King Philip III, son of Philip II, recalled Onate to Mexico City to answer charges. But Onate, unaware of the order, resigned his post in 1607 because he was in such financial difficulty. He did remain in New Mexico to see the town of Santa Fe established and returned to Mexico City in 1608. In a letter to the king, he stated that his feelings had been greatly hurt because the deserters from the colony had not been punished. He also said that the devil had been responsible for all his troubles in New Mexico.

For a time after the fiasco at San Juan Pueblo, Spain ordered all exploration in New Mexico to stop, but then thought better of the decision. In 1609 a new governor for the territory was appointed and some 7,000 Native Americans were baptized into the Catholic faith.

The trial and aftermath

Onate, however, was not allowed to go quietly into the night. In 1613 he was put on trial for crimes committed while acting as governor of the New Mexico colony. These included cruelty, immorality, and false reporting. The most serious of the charges concerned treatment of the Acoma people.

On one of his treasure hunts in 1599, Onate had encountered the Acoma people in west central New Mexico. They lived in what is known as "sky city" in terraced dwellings of stone and **adobe** sitting atop a 357-foot (109-meter) high, flat-topped mountain called a **butte.** Essentially farmers and pottery makers, the Acoma are believed to have inhabited that area since the 10th century. Coronado said that the Acoma had the strongest defensive position in the world. Today access to sky city is gained either by a staircase that has been cut into the rock or by a roadway. About three miles from sky city is another butte, known as katzimo, or Enchanted **Mesa,** which the Aztecs believed to be the dwelling place of their nature gods.

Onate's encounter with the Acoma lasted three terrible days. The Spaniards said it began on the steep northern edge of the rock when the Acomas killed thirteen members of their scouting party. The Acomas said it began in revenge for their refusal to give food and supplies to the invading Spanish. It turned into a marathon of rage and firepower high above the desert floor. Apparently Acoma was used as an example of what would happen to those who disobeyed Onate. He decided to destroy the Acomas' greatest fortress. When the battle ended, 24 of the Acoma men survived. They were sentenced to 20 years of slavery and each had a foot cut off. The Acoma women and children who survived were also enslaved.

Today the descendants of the Acoma still speak of that terrible battle. Catholic priests still serve mass in the huge adobe church that the Acomas were forced to build after their defeat. They try to look at the **atrocities** as the kind of punishment normally practiced by invading armies in the 1500s. Certainly that type of brutality was reality in many European countries of the time.

Onate was found guilty of his crimes and banished from the New Mexico colony forever and from Mexico itself for four years. He was also fined and stripped of his titles and honors. Still fighting his conviction, Onate spent the rest of his life trying to get back his honor. He did eventually return to Spain

Pueblo of Acoma is the oldest continuously inhabited city in the United States.

where the king relented enough to give him the position of mining inspector. He died in Spain in June 1626.

Besides his explorations, Juan de Onate can perhaps be credited with bringing the cowboy to the southwest. The first cowboys in New Mexico may have stemmed from his expedition in 1598. The word "cowboy" actually evolved from the Spanish word, vaquero. The word vaca means "cow." These rugged horsemen had a profound impact on the history of the American southwest and became a romantic legend that continues to the present day.

Juan de Onate was by all reports a brutal man in a place and time not particularly known for kind and gentle acts. But to one degree or another the same can be said about most of the early explorers. Having been taught that native peoples were their inferiors, these explorers showed little conscience about outright brutality to gain their objectives. It is a lesson still being learned today.

As for his accomplishments, Onate earned a place in history as the first European to establish a permanent colony in the southwest. He was also a pioneer in opening the vast region to all the explorers and settlers who would soon follow.

Chapter Six

Junipero Serra
A New Kind of Settlement (1769–1782)

In the very early years of exploration in the Americas, most European countries were looking for treasure or new territory to add to their kingdoms. Later on they began to think about sending some of their own people overseas to live in settlements or colonies owned by the home country. But most of these settlers were still interested mainly in riches or in securing whatever lands the country had already claimed. Junipero Serra (1713–1784) had something else in mind. Devoutly religious, he dreamed of establishing missions in the Americas for the sole purpose of converting the native peoples to the Roman Catholic Church. From 1769 to 1782, Serra founded nine such missions from San Diego to San Francisco, earning him the title of Apostle of California. The Catholic Church made him a saint in 1988 and considers Serra one of its greatest **missionaries.** In addition to the main purpose of **conversion,** Serra's religious settlements strengthened Spain's hold on Alta (Upper) California.

The early dream

Miguel Jose Serra was born on November 24, 1713, in the small town of Petra, Majorca. He spent his first 35 years on that Mediterranean island off the north-

A portrait of Junipero Sera (1713–1784)

eastern coast of Spain. His mother and father, Margarita Ferrer and Antonio Serra, were farmers. Of their five children, only Miguel and Juana, his older sister, lived to adulthood. Little is known about Serra's early life. He was a frail youth who preferred study to strenuous play. He might have been schooled during his early years at the Franciscan church of San Bernadino near his home. Later, Serra apparently moved to Palma, Majorca's capital, to study philosophy at the convent of St. Francis. Despite some worries about his health, he was accepted into the Franciscan order at the age of sixteen. At his confirmation, he took the name Juniper, after Brother Juniper who was the legendary friend of Saint Francis of Assisi, known for his charitable works and dedication to poverty.

Serra became a most devout and dedicated student. Long hours of his day were spent in prayer. This intense devotion to his faith would characterize his work as a missionary. He became a brother in 1731 and in 1742 earned his doctorate from the Lullian University of Palma. When he began to teach theology, one of his first students was another **friar,** Francisco Palou, who later became Serra's biographer and traveled with him to Mexico.

Over the next several years, Serra began to earn a reputation as a fine orator and scholar. But even with his

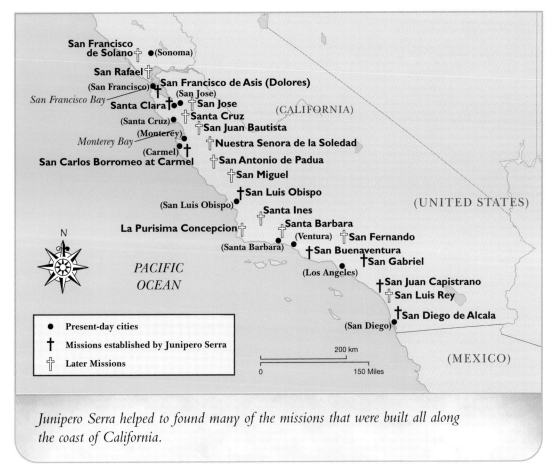

Junipero Serra helped to found many of the missions that were built all along the coast of California.

An aqueduct runs through the city of Queretaro, Mexico.

rewarding career, the priest was not happy. He had long dreamed of working as a **missionary** in the Americas, and now he felt as if his academic life was keeping him from his goal. That all changed in 1748.

On to the first mission

In 1748 Father Mezquia, a priest who was seeking recruits to build missions in Mexico, visited the university where Serra taught. Father Rafael Verger, a colleague of Serra's, decided to go. He was given permission to take two younger **friars** with him. Serra and Palou begged for the chance and Verger accepted them.

Serra left for Mexico shortly after the Easter holiday in 1749. He made a vow to go to the New World and never return. He almost did not make it there. The voyage was extremely rough, but he arrived in Mexico City on January 1, 1750, at the Apostolic College of San Fernando. He was ready and eager to begin his career as a missionary.

But Serra did not care for the relative opulence of Mexico City and wanted to work among the most poor. About five months later he left for Sierra Gorda near Queretaro, north of Mexico City. The native peoples of Sierra Gorda were reported to be the poorest and least friendly in the region, possibly because Sierra Gorda was said to have the unhealthiest climate in the region. But Serra was eager to get started.

Junipero Serra managed to survive for nine years among the unfriendly Native Americans of Sierra Gorda. He converted some of them to Catholicism, learned a little of their language, and taught them about agriculture. In 1758 Serra was ordered to Texas on a most difficult assignment. No successful missions had taken hold there so far.

Serra eagerly awaited a new challenge, but before he could leave the Tonkawa Indians attacked and destroyed the mission near present-day Menard, Texas. The Church decided it was too dangerous to send Serra at that time.

The first California mission

Serra went back to missionary work in Mexico City. But in 1767 events back in Spain would change the course of his life and his dream of founding missions in the New World.

The Mission Nuestra Senora de Loreto is located in Baja California.

King Charles III had taken the Spanish throne in 1759. Charles himself had a mission. He was convinced of his destiny to restore Spain to its position as a first-rate power, a position that Spain had gradually been losing. The survival of Spain as a colonial power in the New World was one of his main objectives. To get what he wanted, both at home and overseas, Charles felt that he must have almost absolute control of the country in order to make what he considered to be necessary reforms. That meant the Church in Spain must be controlled by the **crown.** Most of all he was annoyed by the Jesuits. He considered their international organization to be a challenge to his authority. Claiming that the Jesuits had instigated riots in Madrid in 1766, he ordered a commission to investigate. He ordered all Jesuit orders to be expelled from Spain and its colonies. That meant Mexico and California.

Accordingly, in 1767 Serra and sixteen other Franciscan monks left the College of San Fernando in Mexico City for Lower California. With Serra named president of all missions in that area, he

Founded in 1769 in what is now San Diego, California, the Mission San Diego de Alcala is still an active parish today.

Serra founded the Mission San Juan Capistrano in November 1776.

and the other priests replaced the now banished Jesuits. Junipero Serra's dream was about to come true.

Serra began work as president of the missions on April 1, 1768, in Loreto. About this time, the visitor general to New Spain (Mexico), Jose de Galvez, drew up a plan to extend the Spanish empire in America. Partly this came about because of rumors that the Russians were expanding eastward and to the south from the Aleutian Islands. Galvez believed he could discourage any Russian advance by establishing a line of missions. They would be built at one

day's horse ride from each other all along the coast from the border of Lower California to Monterey, which had been visited by Sebastian Vizcaino in 1602. Serra, who was growing discouraged with military interference in the missions of Lower California, was only too happy to join the voyage north. He dreamed of establishing as many as 50 missions along the coast.

Two expeditions—one by sea and one by land—set out for Alta (Upper) California in 1769. Serra was part of the second and larger land expedition commanded by Don Gaspar de Portola.

Native Americans gather at the San Miguel mission.

It was a struggle to cross the arid desert land, especially for Serra, who had developed swelling and severe pains in one leg. He had been suffering from this condition ever since arriving in Mexico, but now the leg was so painful and so swollen that he could hardly stand. Portola considered sending him back, but Serra's leg improved enough for him to continue. When the expedition reached San Diego, however, he was left behind with others who were ill. Portola continued on to Monterey.

On July 16, 1769, Serra founded the mission of San Diego de Alcala. It was the first mission in California, the first of

9 established by Serra, and the first of 21 eventually built along the coast.

Serra's first months in San Diego were difficult. At times conflict with the Native Americans was deadly. But the frail Franciscan was strong willed in his determination to make the mission succeed. Over the next fifteen years, Serra would establish eight more missions along the coast. In early 1770 a supply ship arrived at San Diego and Serra was able to sail on it to Monterey. On June 3 he founded his second mission, Carmel at Monterey, which became his headquarters. The others were San Antonio and San Gabriel (near

An illustration shows the funeral of Junipero Serra.

the administration in Mexico, which was often lax about sending money and supplies to keep the missions going. Some say that had not the authorities finally listened to Serra and sent money and necessary supplies in 1783, Spain's hold on California would have been lost.

By the end of 1783, several months before his death, some 6,000 Native Americans had been baptized in the missions and the annual harvests took in about 30,000 bushels of grain and vegetables. In addition the native peoples were instructed in the craft of wood working and tending to livestock. The mission workshops produced many of the material goods that were needed at the time in California.

Growing increasingly ill and more frail, Serra grew more determined than ever to continue his work. But he died on August 28, 1784, at his headquarters mission in Monterey. His friend Palou was at his side. Serra was given a funeral at the mission that was elaborate for the time and place.

Junipero Serra is credited with strengthening the Spanish presence in California and opening what became the 31st state to settlers. He introduced cattle, sheep, grains, and fruit from Mexico into California. But he was not without controversy. He strongly supported fair treatment of native peoples and was an ardent foe of prejudice. Yet in the 20th century, Native Americans have charged that, for all the good he did, Serra was also part

Los Angeles) in 1771, San Luis Obispo in 1772, Mission Dolores in San Francisco and San Juan Capistrano in 1776, Santa Clara in 1777, and San Buenaventura in 1782.

His life's work

Serra's leg problems continued, as did his work. He frequently traveled up and down the coast visiting his missions and administering to their needs. By all reports, he was warmly welcomed by his fellow priests and the local people. But Serra frequently ran into trouble with

A statue stands in remembrance of Father Junipero Serra.

of the colonial system, and therefore helped to enslave their ancestors. Indeed, although Serra campaigned for property rights for Native Americans who converted to the Catholic faith, he opposed their right of self-government. He also supported capital punishment, requesting from the Spanish authorities the right to beat Native Americans who disobeyed Spanish laws.

Toward sainthood

Serra became a controversial figure in the Catholic Church as well. In 1985 he was designated as "venerable" by Pope John Paul II. This is a first step toward canonization, or being designated as a saint. To be considered for sainthood, a person must have led a life of heroic sanctity and must have performed at least two miracles. Some activists claimed that considering Serra for sainthood was the same as endorsing the colonization of Native Americans. However most praise his devotion to duty and his staunch defense of the rights of native peoples.

Junipero Serra was declared a saint of the Roman Catholic Church on September 25, 1988. There are many memorials to this frail, iron-willed **missionary,** including a statue in the capitol in Washington, D.C., unveiled on March 1, 1931. There is also a bronze statue in San Francisco's Golden Gate Park, and a granite monument stands in Monterey. They honor the first missionary-explorer in California.

Francisco Silvestre Velez de Escalante and Francisco Dominguez

On the Road to Monterey (1776–1777)

The Grand Canyon in northern Arizona was carved by the Colorado River.

The Escalante River runs through the town of Escalante, Utah. Other sites in Utah and Colorado also carry the name of the Spanish Franciscan **missionary**-explorer, Francisco Silvestre Velez de Escalante. Along with his superior, Francisco Dominguez, Escalante sought a route from Santa Fe (now in New Mexico) to Monterey, on the California coast, in 1776–1777. During their search, the two **friars** explored the southwest region, saw the Grand Canyon, traveled through western Colorado, and were, by some accounts, the first Europeans to explore what is now the state of Utah.

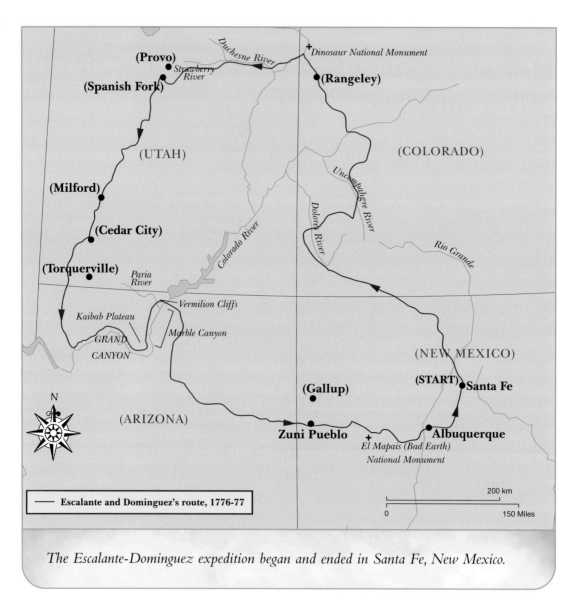

The Escalante-Dominguez expedition began and ended in Santa Fe, New Mexico.

Spanish expansion

At the time of the Escalante and Dominguez expedition, Charles III still sat on the throne of Spain and still wanted to expand Spain's power and influence in the Americas. But the king had not been doing well. Several years earlier, in 1761, England and France were engaged in the so-called Seven Years' War (1759–1763), or the French and Indian War, as it was known in North America. The two countries were mostly battling over colonial territory.

Fearing a British victory, which would upset the balance of power in the New World, Charles signed what was called a Family Compact with France. Both countries were ruled by branches of the Bourbon family, one of the greatest of Europe's **dynasties.** Naturally this brought Spain into the war. But Charles had badly overestimated the strength of France and his own forces. As a result, Spain lost Florida to England.

Charles wanted very much to strengthen his hold on western North America. In the 1770s Spain's colonial empire stretched from Panama north through Mexico and across the American southwest to California. Yet, little was known about this vast territory except that a good deal of it was desert. It was also dangerous, mostly due to some unfriendly native peoples and the treacherous Colorado River, which rises in the western mountains of Colorado and flows for 1,450 miles (2,334 kilometers) into northwestern Mexico. The twisting, rushing river waters have cut remarkably deep trenches into the land, the most spectacular being the Grand Canyon in northwestern Arizona.

The Spanish government wanted to build overland routes through the desert lands to the California coast. This would bring Spain's holdings closer together, which would in turn help to safeguard them from Native American attacks. In 1775 Juan Bautista de Anza explored northern Mexico across the Sonoran Desert, finally reaching Monterey on the California coast by a southern overland route. Now Silvestre Velez de Escalante and Francisco Dominguez would try to find a northern route to Monterey across the Great Basin Desert.

Escalante's plan

Little is known about the personal lives of these **missionary**-explorers. Escalante was born in Spain and had been living in New Mexico for some time when the expedition began. In 1775 he was attending to the needs of native peoples at Zuni and also visited Hopi villages. Dominguez, a native of Mexico, had been asked by his Franciscan superiors to inspect missions in New Mexico. Both men had long been interested in trying to find a safe route to missions in California.

Escalante and Dominguez met for the first time in Santa Fe at the request of Governor Don Pedro Fermin de Mendinueta. Escalante presented a plan for the expedition, which the governor approved. It called for fourteen men to **trek** north of the Grand Canyon. They hoped to avoid hostile native peoples, as well as the most difficult desert lands. The more direct northwest route would have taken them through the land of Chirumas, who were reported to be a cannibalistic people. North of the Grand Canyon was the territory of the far friendlier Utes. From there they would follow a course due west to California and Monterey. Probably because Escalante was the one who

A drawing shows Santa Fe as it appeared in the 1800s.

initiated the plan, his name is usually given first in any report of the expedition by the two missionaries. However, Dominguez, being Escalante's superior, was actually in charge of the journey, and the resulting **journal** was kept by both men.

The expedition was planned for July 4, 1776. However, a Comanche attack in the area sent Escalante off to administer to the injured. Then he was forced to take to his bed with severe side pains, probably a kidney ailment. He would die in 1780 of kidney disease. Some records say he was only 30 years old.

The expedition begins

Finally, the expedition began on July 29, 1776, from Santa Fe. The party of fourteen included two members of the Timpanogot tribe who would serve as guides. They were known as Silvestre and Joaquin. Joaquin was only twelve years old and he led the party throughout the entire journey. An equally important member was Bernado Miera y Pachecho, a retired military engineer. Miera's maps following the expedition provided the first drawings of what became the state of Utah.

No one in the party knew very much about the region they were entering. Traveling to the northwest, they reached and named the winding Dolores River on August 13. After setting up camp, Escalante and Dominguez explored the area. They noted in their journal the ruins of a small Native American village above the camp. Now called Escalante Ruin, it is the first written record of a prehistoric Anasazi site in Colorado. Another nearby site, uncovered in modern times, is known as the Dominguez Ruin.

Next, they moved north through western Colorado. At one point they became so hopelessly lost and without water that death seemed certain. They were rescued by a Ute Native American who took them to his own camp on the Uncompahgre River. From there they were guided north to the site of present-day Rangely, Colorado, near the Utah border.

Over 2,000 natural sandstone arches stand in Utah's Arches National park.

Entering Utah

Feeling reasonably certain that they were out of reach of the dreaded Chirumas, the party now turned west and entered Utah near Dinosaur National Monument. Since food was always scarce, they were encouraged by the sight of a lone bison, which gave them a fresh supply of meat. They were also fearful of the Shoshone people in the territory.

It was mid-September. The two Ute guides were leading them toward their own homeland in Utah Valley. They crossed the Duchesne and Strawberry Rivers in what is now Duschesne County and pressed on to the home of the Timpanogots. Several days later they followed the Spanish Fork River to the mouth of Spanish Fork Canyon, where they climbed a hill to look down on the valley. They finally camped on the shores of Utah Lake at the mouth of the Provo River, south of present-day Provo, Utah.

The valley was a truly breathtaking place. Both **missionaries** wrote glowing journal reports about the glorious spot that would be ideal for establishing a colony. There was a plentiful water supply, lots of timber in the nearby mountains, good grazing land, animals to hunt, and fish to catch. There seemed to be enough room for all the people now living in New Mexico. And the Native Americans, who were then the biggest concentration of people in the territory, seemed friendly to the newcomers. They were so friendly, in fact, that the two priests promised they would return in a year to teach the gospel. They also promised to bring crops and cattle. It was a promise they could not keep.

The missionary-explorers reluctantly left the Utah Valley. They also left behind Silvestre, who had promised to lead them only as far as his home. Along with Joaquin and a new guide, whom they called Jose Maria, they turned to the southwest, traveling roughly along the route that is now Interstate 15. Just north of present-day Milford, Utah, they suffered some internal trouble. A fight broke out between one of the Spaniards and his servant. This frightened the new guide, Jose Maria, and he left the party to return home. It was October 5.

The perilous route

The expedition continued to the southwest. Miera the mapmaker calculated their position by the stars. He reasoned that by turning directly west at what is now Cedar City in southwestern Utah, the party would reach Monterey **Bay.** Miera's calculations were generally farther north than the expedition actually was, so had they taken that route, they would have reached the California coast closer to present-day San Jose or San Francisco than Monterey. They would have had to cross southern Nevada, enter California, and head over the Sierra Nevada to the coast.

On the day of Jose Maria's desertion, a fierce snowstorm hit the camp. Imprisoned until the storm passed, the explorers sloshed through the snow-drifts with great difficulty. The freezing temperatures and snowstorms brought them to the point of despair. Perhaps it was the loss of a guide, perhaps it was the realization that winter was fast setting in, or perhaps it was the terrible conditions. Perhaps it was all three of these things. In any case, Escalante and Dominguez decided that the search for the route to Monterey should be abandoned. They had come far and suffered through terrible hardships, but it seemed fool-ish to continue.

On October 8 the priests announced their decision to the rest of the group and met with resistance. A number of the party had agreed to the expedition only in the expectation of the riches they would receive for opening a route to Monterey. They threatened a mutiny. This caused Escalante and Domin-guez to reconsider for a few days. But reason overcame them again, and Dominguez told the group that it would be suicide to continue that

The Paria River is now part of the Grand Staircase-Escalante National Monument in Utah.

season. They must return to Santa Fe. In fact the priests were now in a hurry to get home so that they could start preparations for another expedition. But the way home proved more terrible than the outgoing journey. The temperatures were bitter. The snow was constant. Food was scarce. When all the cattle were eaten, the mules were next.

Their course was south through Cedar Valley, down Ash Creek, and across the Virgin River near modern-day Toquerville, Utah. There they encountered some friendly Paiutes who gave them nuts and berries.

Skirting the rugged walls of the Grand Canyon, the expedition took a week to cross northern Arizona through the Kaibab Plateau and follow the base of the Vermillion Cliffs to the Paria River. It took another eleven days before they reached the Colorado, which they crossed near Marble Canyon. The site is now called the Crossing of the Fathers.

At one time it was a noted historical site because the priests had carved steps out of the canyon wall. The steps are now covered by 500 feet (152 meters) of water in the Lake Powell reservoir.

It was November 26 before Escalante and Dominguez reached a settled community again south of Gallup, New Mexico, at the Zuni **Pueblo.** They worked on the **journal** of the expedition before moving on. On their way east, they stopped at what is now El Mapais (The Bad Earth) National Monument.

Traveling to the east, they reached Sante Fe on January 2, 1777. The next day they reported to the governor.

The two missionary-explorers had traveled more than 1,700 miles (2,736 kilometers) on a six-and-a-half month journey to nowhere. They never came anywhere near their goal of Monterey. They had instead traveled in a huge circle around the southwest. They had endured incredible hardships and dangers they would never forget.

By most accounts the expedition of Escalante and Dominguez has to be called a failure. They did not find a northern route from Sante Fe to Monterey. They did not even reach California. They could not keep the promise they had made to return to the beautiful Utah Valley. They did try, however. But when they requested funding for a mission, they were told that "the government has effected a retrenchment policy." That meant the Spanish king was not spending any more money on extending missions into new and distant lands. Utah's history might have been far different had Escalante and Dominguez been allowed to continue their work. The Utah landscape might be dotted with Spanish names like the state of New Mexico. Had the Spanish already been there, Brigham Young, who was looking for a place to establish his Mormon church, might not have settled around what is now Salt Lake City.

The priests' glowing descriptions of the Utah Valley fell on deaf ears, too. Perhaps the king decided it was just too expensive and too risky to send settlers into such an unknown place.

Escalante and Dominguez are noted in some accounts as the first white explorers in Utah. That is disputed by some historians. In 1889 Hubert Howe Bancroft reported in his History of Utah that Don Garcia Lopez de Cardenas, a lieutenant under Coronado, traveled from the Hopi villages of northeastern Arizona in 1540 and crossed into southeastern Utah. He reported being stopped by the great canyon of the Colorado River. But there is no such canyon in that part of Utah, so historians doubted his claim. In 1940 it was decided that Cardenas had traveled west from the Hopi village, not north.

Some researchers now say that Juan Maria Antonio Rivera was the first European explorer to enter southeastern Utah around Moab, in 1765. The second edition of *The Utah Guide,* by Allan Kent Powell, also gives the honor to Rivera. Whether or not Escalante and Dominguez were the first in Utah, they did add another dimension to the growing knowledge about the vast and unknown territory that became the southwestern United States. The maps drawn by Miera proved invaluable. Years later, they would guide a new group of explorers along what became known as the Old Spanish Trail all the way to the coast of California.

Epilogue:

What Did They Find?

The story of exploration in the southwestern United States is to a large extent a story of Spain, of Spanish explorers and Spanish **missionaries.** It is because of men such as Coronado, Vizcaino, and Serra that the southwest is dotted with names like San Diego, Monterey, and Santa Fe. The southwestern United States retains a decidedly Spanish flavor even today.

For the great majority of the conquistadors from Spain and explorers from other European nations, the main reasons for expeditions to the Americas were gold, power, and status. Spain also claimed a concern with what it saw as a moral issue. It became Spain's duty to make conquests of what it regarded as heathen, or non-Christian, people and convert them to the Roman Catholic religion. That is why Spain sent along missionaries and **friars** on expeditions to North and South America. The friars themselves, men such as Junipero Serra, were dedicated to "rescuing" the so-called heathens. Thousands of Native Americans were converted to Christianity during the period of exploration and colonization by Spain. However, many native peoples had no desire to be converted and certainly resented being forced into near slavery in order to be "saved."

From the time of Marcos de Niza in 1539 to the time of the missionaries Francisco Escalanate and Francisco Dominguez in 1776–1777, much had changed in what Europeans thought of as the New World. A good deal of northeastern America had been explored by men such as Amerigo Vespucci and Martin Frobisher. Marquette and Jolliet had traveled the mighty Mississippi River, and Robert LaSalle had located the Gulf of Mexico. Ponce de Leon had claimed Florida and Pedro de Aviles had founded St. Augustine, the oldest city in the United States. By the time Escalante and Dominguez sought a northern route to Monterey **Bay** in 1776–1777, thirteen colonies on the eastern coast had decided to rebel against their English rulers and form a new country, which became the United States of America. From that time on, the ruling colonial powers would begin to lose their hold on North America.

A new world was forming. Much of what it became was built on the travels and expeditions of the early explorers. Some of them were well meaning and dedicated. Some of them were cruel glory-seekers. But each one had a part to play, for better or for worse, in the development of the New World.

Important Events in the Exploration of the Southwestern United States

1520   Juan Cabrillo joins Cortes in assault on Aztec capital

1523   Cabrillo is part of Spanish conquest of Central America

1535   Francisco Coronado travels to New Spain as aide to Antonio de Mendoza

1538   Coronado is named governor of Neuva Galacia

1539   Marcos de Niza claims to find seven golden cities of Cibola

1540   Coronado leaves for Cibola; instead finds **adobe** houses of the Zuni tribe

1541   Coronado sees buffalo herds on his unsuccessful expedition to Quivira

1542   Coronado returns to Mexico; Cabrillo leads expedition along the Pacific coast

1546   Coronado is found innocent of charges of cruelty

1587   Sebastian Vizcaino is aboard the pirated ship *Santa Ana* off the California coast

1593   Vizcaino forms expedition company

1596   Vizcaino sails in three ships to explore California coast

1598   Juan de Onate establishes colony of New Mexico for Spain

1599   Onate encounters Acoma people

1601   Onate looks for Quivira

1602   Vizcaino begins second voyage along California coast, May 5; sights Monterey **Bay,** December 15

1603   Vizcaino sights Cape Mendocino; misses San Francisco Bay, January 12

1606   Onate is recalled to Mexico City

1607   Onate resigns his post as governor

1613   Onate is put on trial on cruelty charges

1749   Junipero Serra leaves for Mexico

1750   Serra arrives in Mexico City, January 1

1766   Charles III of Spain expels Jesuits from Spain and its colonies

1767   Serra leaves for California

1768   Serra begins the work of building missions along California coast

1769   Serra joins expedition to establish missions and explore the coast

1770   Carmel mission is founded, June 3

1771   San Antonio and San Gabriel missions are established

1772   San Luis Obispo mission is established

1776   Serra establishes missions at San Francisco and San Juan Capistrano; Friars Escalante and Dominguez begin journey to find northern route from Santa Fe to Monterey Bay; they are perhaps the first Europeans to enter Utah

1777   Escalante and Dominguez return from unsuccessful expedition, January 2; mission at Santa Clara is founded by Serra

1782   Last of Serra's missions is founded at San Buenaventura (Ventura, Calif.)

Glossary

adobe brick or building material made of sun-dried earth

armor defensive covering for the body, as a soldier

artillery various weapons of an army

atrocity wicked, brutal, cruel act

bay inlet of the sea

buffalo large, shaggy-maned mammal (also called a bison)

butte isolated hill with steep sides; see mesa

channel bed where a natural stream of water runs

conversion to bring about a change, generally in religious beliefs

crown imperial or royal power

dynasty succession of rulers in the same line of descent

fishery place for catching fish or other sea animals

flagship generally the largest ship of a fleet, carrying the commander

forgery crime of falsely altering or creating a fake document or check

friar member of a religious order

galleon square-rigged sailing ship especially used by the Spanish in the 15th to 18th centuries

journal written account of day-to-day events

missionary one who undertakes the work of spreading religious beliefs

mesa isolated flat-topped hill or mountain, usually larger than a butte

pueblo communal dwelling of a Native American village in the southwestern United States

sloop sailboat with one mast

strait passageway, usually narrow, connecting two bodies of water

trek long journey, especially one involving great difficulties

uprising act of many people in defiance of authority

viceroy governor of a colony or province who represents the king or sovereign of the ruling country

Further Reading

Baker, Daniel B. (ed.). *Explorers and Discovers of the World*. Detroit: Gale, 1993.

Bankston, John. *Juan Rodriguez Cabrillo*. Bear, Del.: Mitchell Lane, 2003.

Bohlander, Richard E. (ed.). *World Explorers and Discoverers*. Cambridge, Mass.: Da Capo, 2003.

Doak, Robin Santos. *Coronado: Francisco Vazques de Coronado Explores the Southwest*. Minneapolis: Compass Point Books, 2001.

Genet, Donna. *Father Junipero Serra: Founder of California Missions*. Berkeley Heights, N.J.: Enslow, 1996.

Otfinoski, Steven. *Francisco Coronado: In Search of the Seven Cities of Gold*. Estes Park, Colo.: Benchmark Investigative Group, 2002.

Index